The Lady
with the Alligator Purse

Adapted and illustrated by
Nadine Bernard Westcott

Joy Street Books

Little, Brown and Company
Boston · Toronto · London

For
Jim and Sandy
Love, Deanie

Copyright © 1988 by Nadine Bernard Westcott

First Edition

Library of Congress Cataloging-in-Publication Data

Westcott, Nadine Bernard.
The lady with the alligator purse.

Summary: The old jump rope/nonsense rhyme features an ailing young Tiny Tim.

1. Jump rope rhymes. 2. Nonsense verses.
3. Children's poetry. [1. Jump rope rhymes.
2. Nonsense verses] I. Title.
PZ8.3.W4998Lad   1988   87-21368
ISBN 0-316-93135-7

10 9 8 7 6 5 4 3 2

Published simultaneously in Canada
by Little, Brown & Company (Canada) Limited
Printed in the United States of America

Miss Lucy had a baby,
His name was Tiny Tim,

She put him in the bathtub
To see if he could swim.

He drank up all the water,
He ate up all the soap,

He tried to eat the bathtub,
But it wouldn't go down his throat.

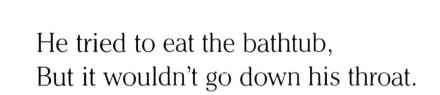

Miss Lucy called the doctor,

Miss Lucy called the nurse,

Miss Lucy called the lady
With the alligator purse.

In came the doctor,
In came the nurse,
In came the lady
With the alligator purse.

"Mumps," said the doctor,

"Measles," said the nurse,

"Nonsense!" said the lady
With the alligator purse.

"Penicillin," said the doctor,

"Castor oil," said the nurse,

"Pizza!" said the lady
With the alligator purse.

Out went the doctor,
Out went the nurse,

Out went the lady
With the alligator purse.